Bible
Questions
and
Answers

Designed and edited by
BOOKWORK

Editor: Annabel Blackledge
Art Director: Jill Plank
Art Editor: Kate Mullins

Bible Consultants: AD Publishing Services, Annette Reynolds

For Kingfisher

Editors: Jonathan Stroud, Russell McLean
Senior Designer: Jane Tassie
DTP Manager: Nicky Studdart
Production Controller: Debbie Otter
Artwork Archivists: Wendy Allison, Steve Robinson

The publishers would like to thank the following artists for their contribution to this book:

Harry Bishop; Gino D'Achille (*Artist Partners Ltd*); Richard Garland; Rob Hefferan (*Advocate*);
John Keay; Michael Langham Rowe; Massimiliano Longo (*Milan Illustrations Agency*);
Kevin Maddison; Chris Molan; Rob Perry (*Advocate*);
Francis Phillipps; Martin Reiner; Nick Spender (*Advocate*)

KINGFISHER
Kingfisher Publications Plc,
New Penderel House,
283–288 High Holborn,
London WC1V 7HZ

www.kingfisherpub.com

First published by Kingfisher Publications Plc in 2002
This paperback edition first published in 2005
2 4 6 8 10 9 7 5 3 1

1TR/0605/LFG/FR(PICA)/150MA/F

Copyright © Kingfisher Publications Plc 2002

All rights reserved. No part of this publication
may be reproduced, stored in a retrieval system
or transmitted by any means, electronic,
mechanical, photocopying or otherwise,
without the prior permission of the publisher.

A CIP catalogue record for this book is
available from the British Library.

ISBN 10: 0 7534 1248 9
ISBN 13: 978 0 7534 1248 0

Printed in China

Bible Questions and Answers

Dennis Doyle

KINGFISHER

Contents

In the beginning	6
Breaking God's rules	8
Noah and the flood	10
Abraham and Isaac	12
Jacob	14
Joseph	16
Moses	18
Plagues in Egypt	20
A freed people	22
A special people	24
The Promised Land	26
Heroes and heroines	28
David	30
Kings and prophets	32
Daniel	34
Jonah and the big fish	36
The birth of Jesus	38
Jesus grows up	40
Friends and disciples	42
Signs and miracles	44

Sermon on the mountain	46	Trial and crucifixion	56
Jesus the storyteller	48	The Resurrection	58
An incredible picnic	50	Working for God	60
Jesus goes to Jerusalem	52	Paul the apostle	62
The Last Supper	54	Index	64

IN THE BEGINNING

What did God create to fill the universe?

First of all God created day and night, the sky, the oceans and the land. God covered the land with all kinds of plants. Next, God made the Sun, Moon and stars. Then God created living creatures to fill the seas, the sky and the land.

Who did God put in charge of the creatures?

God made a man called Adam and a woman called Eve. He put them in charge of the fish in the sea, the birds in the sky and the animals on the land. God was very pleased with everything that had been created.

Where did Adam and Eve live?

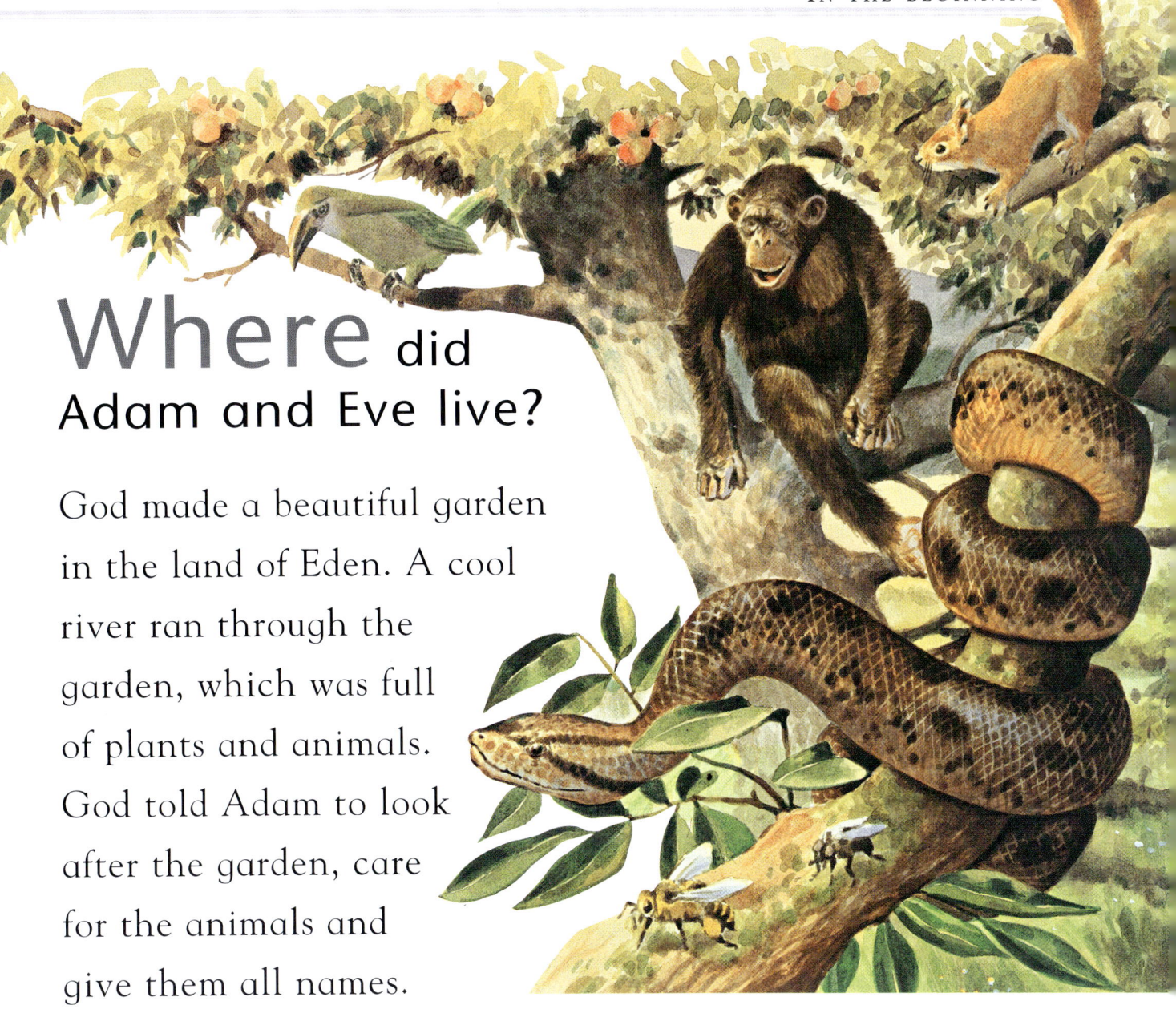

God made a beautiful garden in the land of Eden. A cool river ran through the garden, which was full of plants and animals. God told Adam to look after the garden, care for the animals and give them all names.

What did God do when the Creation was finished?

God made everything in six days. On the seventh day, God rested. God blessed that day and said that it was special. It would be a holy day for ever more, to mark the creation of the world. It is now known as the Sabbath day.

Who tempted Eve to disobey God?

God told Adam and Eve that they could eat anything in the garden, except the fruit from one special tree. But Eve was tricked by a crafty serpent. The serpent said that if Adam and Eve ate the forbidden fruit they would become as clever as God. The fruit looked so good that Eve ate some, despite God's warning. She offered some to Adam and he ate it too.

What did Adam and Eve do after eating the fruit?

Adam and Eve were frightened that God would be angry with them, because they had broken the rule about eating the special fruit. They were so ashamed that they tried to hide, but God found them and asked them why they had ignored the warning. Adam blamed Eve and she blamed the serpent, but God told them both to leave the garden.

Why did Adam and Eve's son Cain kill his brother Abel?

Cain and Abel each gave God a gift. Cain gave some of the crops he had grown, and Abel gave some of his best animals. God was especially pleased with Abel's offering, and this made Cain very jealous. He went with his brother to a field and killed him there. God was angry with Cain and punished him by telling him that his life would always be hard.

Noah and the flood

Why did God send a flood to destroy the world?

Almost everyone in the world had become wicked. They disobeyed God all the time. God grew very angry, and began to wish that all these people had never been created. It was clear that they would not change their wicked ways, so God sent a great flood to destroy them.

Why did God tell Noah to build an ark?

God saw that Noah was a good man, and decided to save him and his family from the flood. God told Noah to build an ark that would float on the waters, and to fill it with animals of every kind.

What did Noah do when the rain stopped?

Noah released a dove from the ark. When it did not return, Noah knew it had found dry land. Noah waited until God told him to leave the ark, then he let out the animals and worshipped God for keeping them all safe.

What promise did God make when all the water had gone?

God made a promise to Noah and all his descendants that a flood would never again be sent to destroy everything on earth. As a special sign of this promise, God put a rainbow in the sky. God told Noah that every time a rainbow appeared in the sky, it would be a reminder of the promise made to all God's people.

ABRAHAM AND ISAAC

Why was Abraham and Sarah's son Isaac so precious to them?

Abraham and Sarah had grown too old to have children – Abraham was one hundred years old and Sarah was ninety. But because Abraham was faithful to God they were promised a son. God said that the child's name would be Isaac and that he would be blessed. This news made Abraham laugh with delight.

How did God test Abraham's faith?

To test Abraham's faith, God asked him to take Isaac, the child he loved more than his own life, and sacrifice him. Abraham trusted God and obeyed, but just as he raised the knife God called out and stopped him. Abraham saw a ram caught in a bush nearby and offered that as a gift to God instead.

How did God reward Abraham for his obedience?

Because Abraham was willing to sacrifice his own son for God's sake, God rewarded him. God told Abraham that he would have a large family, and leave behind him as many descendants as there are stars in the heavens and grains of sand on the seashore. God promised to bless Abraham's family and look after them throughout their lives.

Who did Isaac marry when he grew up?

Abraham gave his servant ten camels and sent him to find Isaac a wife. After weeks of travelling, the servant came to a well. He stopped and asked God for help. God sent a girl called Rebecca to the well. She gave the servant a drink of water, and offered to fetch some for his camels too. This was a sign that God had chosen Rebecca to be Isaac's wife.

How were Isaac's twin sons Jacob and Esau different from each other?

Esau, the first twin to be born, was his father's favourite. He had rough, red skin and was covered with thick hair. Esau grew up to be adventurous and a skilled hunter. Jacob, the second twin, was born holding on to Esau's heel. He was gentle and quiet, and he spent most of his time at home. As time passed, Jacob began to grow jealous of his twin brother.

How did Jacob trick his father?

When Isaac was old and close to death, he sent for Esau so that he could give him a blessing. First, he asked his favourite son to go out hunting and bring him back some meat. But while Esau was gone, Rebecca prepared some meat of her own. She told Jacob to cover himself with goat hair and take the meat to his father. Isaac, who was nearly blind, was fooled and gave his blessing to Jacob instead of Esau.

What did Jacob dream about when he slept at Bethel?

Jacob dreamed of a ladder that led from earth to Heaven, with angels going up and down the steps. He dreamt that God stood beside him and told him that he and his relatives would be successful and would one day own the land where he slept. When Jacob woke up, he could still feel God's presence all around him.

Who did Jacob wrestle with on his way back to Canaan?

A man appeared before Jacob and began to wrestle with him. Jacob clung to the stranger until he begged to be released. Jacob asked him for a blessing, but the stranger simply told him to change his name to Israel – he who struggles with God.

How did Jacob show that Joseph was his favourite son?

Jacob had twelve sons and one daughter. Joseph, who was born when Jacob was an old man, was his favourite child. Jacob showed Joseph how special he was by giving him a wonderful ornamental coat of many different colours. This made Jacob's brothers very jealous.

Who threw Joseph down a deep well?

Joseph's brothers decided to kill him because they believed he wanted to have power over them. Reuben, the oldest brother, had second thoughts and persuaded them not to kill him. The brothers threw Joseph into a dry well, then sold him as a slave to passing merchants.

What happened to Joseph when he was sold as a slave?

Joseph was taken to Egypt and sold to Potiphar, the captain of Pharaoh's guards. God looked after Joseph, and he became head of the household. But Potiphar's wife became angry when Joseph refused to fall in love with her. She pretended that Joseph had attacked her, and Potiphar put Joseph in prison.

Why did Pharaoh free Joseph from prison?

While Joseph was in prison, he explained to two of Pharaoh's men the meaning of their dreams. Years later, Pharaoh himself had dreams that he did not understand. One of his men remembered Joseph's skill. Joseph was brought from prison to explain the dreams, and Pharaoh made him one of his most powerful leaders. Joseph rode around the city in a golden chariot.

Why did the Israelites become slaves in Egypt?

For many years, the Israelites were welcome in Egypt. They were given good land, and they prospered until long after Joseph's death. But eventually there were so many Israelites that the Egyptians began to worry that they would take over their country. So they made the Israelites into slaves.

Why did Moses' mother hide him in a basket?

In an attempt to keep the Israelites under control, the Egyptians began killing Israelite boys. Moses' mother put him in a basket and hid him in the reeds beside the River Nile. Miriam, his sister, stood and watched. An Egyptian princess found Moses, and sent Miriam to find an Israelite woman to help her care for the baby. Miriam returned with her own mother.

Why did Moses flee from Egypt?

When Moses was a young man, he saw an Egyptian beating an Israelite slave. This made Moses so angry that he killed the Egyptian and hid the body. Later, he saw two Israelites fighting and stepped in to stop them. The men were scared. They asked Moses whether he was going to kill them too. Moses began to worry that Pharaoh also knew about the murder, so he ran away.

Who spoke to Moses from a burning bush?

Moses was looking after his sheep when he noticed a burning bush. The fire did not seem to be harming the bush, so Moses decided to take a closer look. Then God spoke to him from within the flames. God asked Moses to go to Pharaoh and demand that the Israelites be set free from slavery. Moses was scared but he knew he should do what God asked of him.

Why did God send plagues on the people of Egypt?

God sent plagues on Egypt because Pharaoh did not set the Israelites free when Moses asked him to. Pharaoh refused to obey because he did not know how powerful God was.

How many plagues did the Egyptians suffer?

God sent ten plagues altogether. First, God turned all the rivers, lakes and drinking water in Egypt into blood. Then God sent a plague of frogs, which filled people's homes and even got into their clothes and their food. Next, God turned the dust into gnats, filled the Egyptians' houses with flies and let their cows, sheep and goats die. All Egyptians became covered in horrible boils, hailstorms flattened their crops and locusts ate what was left. Then God brought darkness to cover the land. The Egyptians could not even see one another, but the Israelites' homes were filled with light.

What was the last and most terrible plague that God sent?

Even after God had sent nine plagues on the people of Egypt, Pharaoh would not free the Israelites. So God killed the first-born children and animals of all Egyptians. God told the Israelites to stay indoors and eat a meal of lamb or goat with bitter herbs. The Israelites painted blood on the doorposts of their homes so that God would pass over and not kill anything inside. This was known as the Passover.

A FREED PEOPLE

What did Pharaoh let the Israelites take with them to freedom?

Pharaoh was terrified by the Passover plague. He told the Israelites to take their sheep, goats and cattle, and leave Egypt quickly. They only just had time to grab their unrisen bread dough before they set off. God had already advised the Israelites to ask the Egyptians for gifts of silver and gold, so they left Egypt with enough livestock and possessions to begin a new life.

How did Moses and his people escape from Pharaoh's army?

God guided Moses and the Israelites as far as the Red Sea, appearing to them as a pillar of cloud by day and a pillar of fire by night. The Egyptian army were chasing close behind them, but God divided the Red Sea's waters in two. The Israelites crossed safely between the walls of water.

What happened to the Egyptian army after the Israelites escaped?

God sent an angel, who caused darkness to fall and slow down Pharaoh's army. But as soon as the Israelites reached the far shore of the Red Sea, the Egyptian army followed them. They had not got far, however, when God caused the wheels of their chariots to get stuck. The soldiers were scared and realized that they were in danger. But before they could turn back, God made the walls of water close up again, drowning all the men in Pharaoh's army.

What rules did God tell the Israelites to obey?

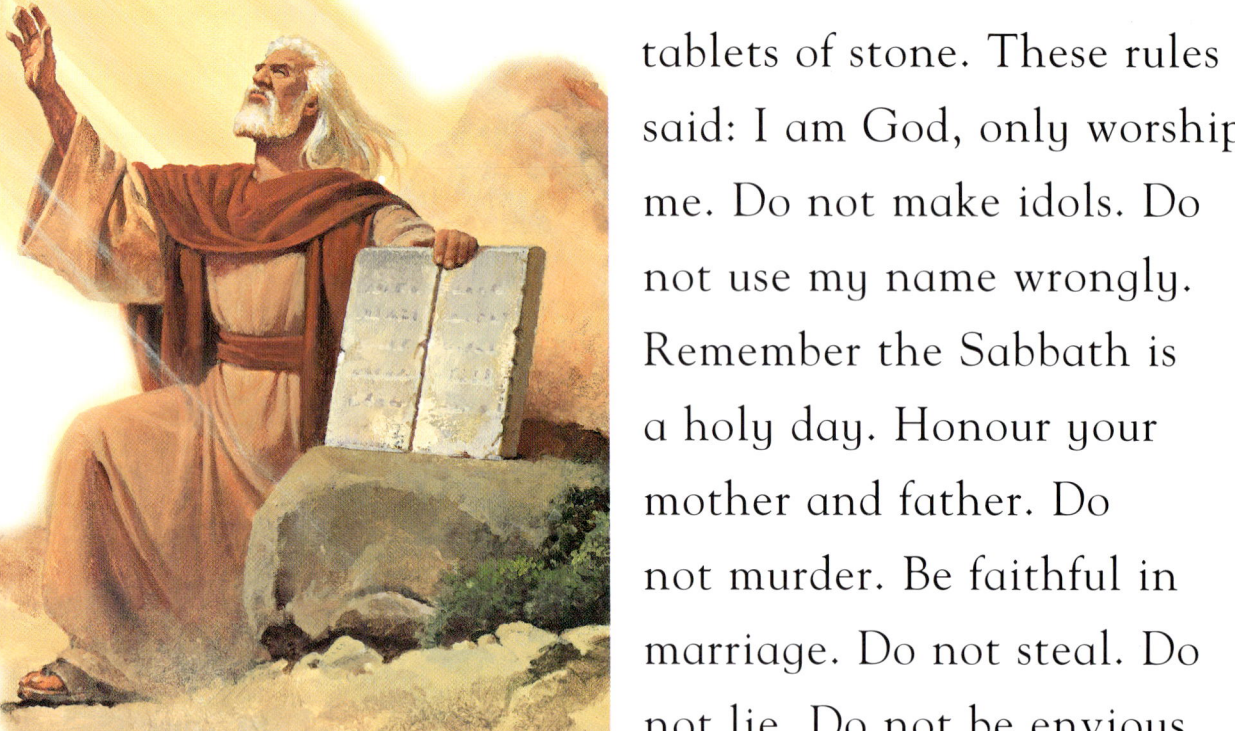

God gave Moses a list of rules called the Ten Commandments, written on two tablets of stone. These rules said: I am God, only worship me. Do not make idols. Do not use my name wrongly. Remember the Sabbath is a holy day. Honour your mother and father. Do not murder. Be faithful in marriage. Do not steal. Do not lie. Do not be envious.

Why did God ask for a holy tent and a holy box?

To help the Israelites understand that God was near and would care for them, God told them to make a box called the Ark of the Covenant to keep the stone tablets in. The Israelites put the Ark in a holy tent called the Tabernacle, creating a sacred place where they could meet with God.

How did the Israelites break the first two commandments?

Moses spent forty days and nights speaking to God about the Ten Commandments. Afraid that he was not going to return, many of the Israelites broke the first two rules. They asked Aaron to build them a new idol. He used their earrings to make a golden calf, and they worshipped it. When he did return, Moses was so angry that he broke the stone tablets in two.

How did God punish the Israelites for their lack of faith?

God said that the Israelites would all be destroyed for their lack of faith, but Moses begged for mercy. God agreed not to kill all of them, but sent a plague on those who had been unfaithful. When the Israelites continued to disobey, God left them wandering in the desert for forty years.

The Promised Land

Why did Moses never reach the Promised Land?

Moses had led God's people for many years, and God had trusted him. But, time and time again, Moses failed to prevent the Israelites disobeying God. God let Moses see the Promised Land before he died, but he chose Moses' general, Joshua, to lead the people into Canaan.

How did Joshua learn about the armies in Canaan?

Joshua sent two spies to the Canaanite city of Jericho to see how strong their armies were. The king of Jericho heard of this and sent men to capture them. A woman called Rahab let the spies hide in her house in the city walls, and helped them to escape by climbing down a rope. When the Israelites invaded the city, they spared the lives of Rahab and her family.

How did Joshua capture the enemy city of Jericho?

God used a miracle to help Joshua capture the ancient city of Jericho. God told the Israelite army to march around the city walls every day for six days, carrying the Ark of the Covenant. Seven priests with trumpets made of rams' horns marched in front of the Ark. On the seventh day, God told Joshua's army to march around the city walls seven times, and told the priests to blow their trumpets. God told the whole army to shout and make a great noise when the trumpets sounded. The Israelites obeyed God and the city walls came tumbling down. Then the army marched in and captured Jericho.

Who was called the Mother of Israel?

Deborah was a great leader in Israel. She sat under a palm tree and used her wisdom to help thousands of people settle their arguments. She also helped the Israelites defeat the Canaanites, bringing peace to the land. She became known as the Mother of Israel.

How did Gideon know he could trust God?

When the Midianites had power over Israel, God chose Gideon to defeat them. To win Gideon's trust, God made some lamb's wool wet with dew although the ground was dry. Then God made the wool dry, but the ground wet. God chose Gideon's army by watching men drink at a pool. Those who stayed alert as they drank were chosen to fight.

How did Samson kill thousands of Philistines?

For many years, the Philistines ruled over Israel. When they killed the wife of the Israelite leader Samson, he rebelled. He killed many of them with a donkey's jawbone, and later many more by pushing down the pillars of their temple.

How did God call Samuel?

When the prophet Samuel was a boy, he was trained for God's work by a priest called Eli. One night, Samuel heard a voice. It called him twice. He thought it was Eli, but Eli said it was God. When God called again, Samuel said, "Speak Lord, for your servant is listening."

How did David help defeat the Philistines?

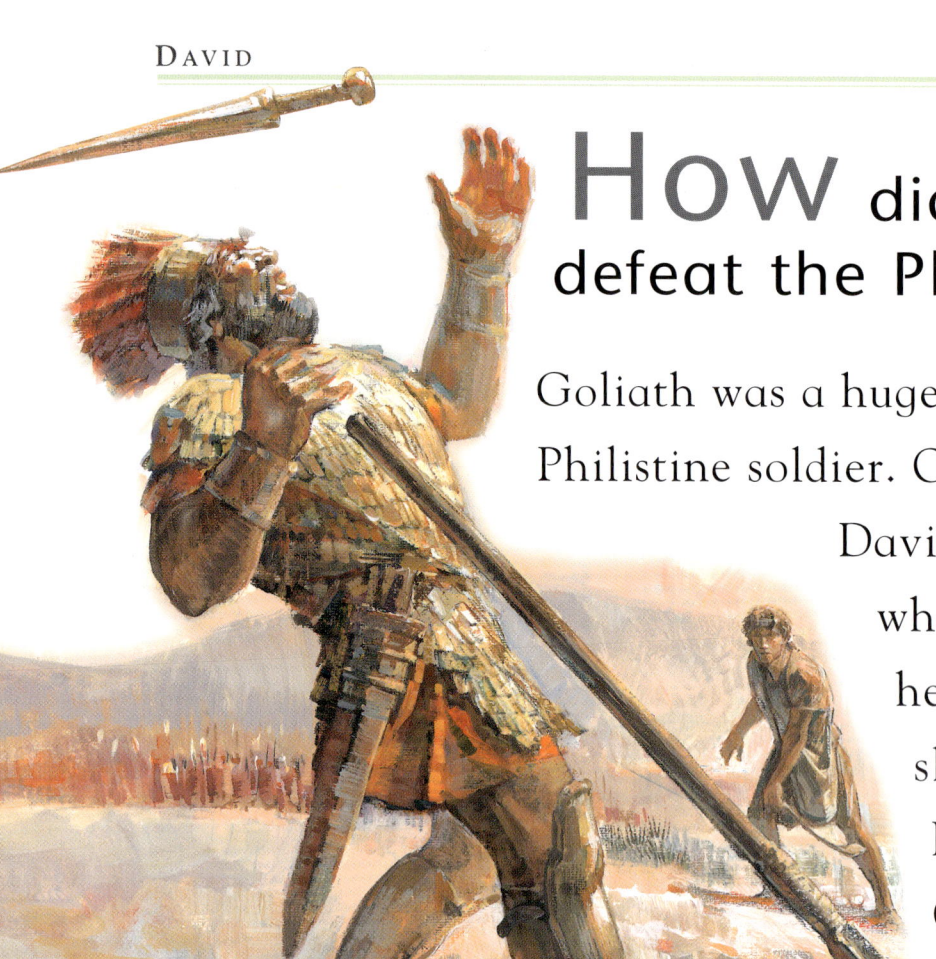

Goliath was a huge and powerful Philistine soldier. Of all the Israelites, David was the only one who trusted God to help him. With only a slingshot for a weapon, David fired a stone at Goliath's head and killed him. Scared by what they had seen, the Philistines fled.

What did King Saul do when he became jealous of David?

David was strong and brave, God was on his side and the Israelites loved him. King Saul became jealous of David, and began to worry that he would steal his kingdom. One day, in a jealous rage, Saul tried to kill David by pinning him to a wall with a spear, but David managed to dodge the spear, and escaped unharmed.

What did David do to show how much he loved God?

When he was thirty years old, David became king of Israel. To show his devotion to God, he brought the Ark of the Covenant to Jerusalem. There was great celebration in the city. David also built a new tent for the Ark, and wrote many of the hymns in the Bible praising God.

How did David's son Absalom die?

David's son Absalom tried to steal David's kingdom. David was sad to fight against his own son, but they went to battle and David won. Absalom escaped, but his long hair got caught in a tree. Joab, the leader of David's army, found him and killed him with three spears.

KINGS AND PROPHETS

What did wise King Solomon build so the people could worship God?

God gave David's son Solomon great wisdom, so he built a magnificent temple in Jerusalem. He employed nearly three hundred thousand people to build the great Temple, and used only the very finest materials. After seven years, when the Temple was finished, David put the Ark in a special, gold-covered room called the Most Holy Place.

How did Elijah prove God's power?

God's prophet Elijah challenged the priests of the god Baal to a contest. He placed a bull on an altar, and told the priests to ask Baal to set it on fire. The priests tried, but nothing happened. Then Elijah prayed to God, and the altar burst into flames. Filled with God's power, Elijah raced the king's chariot back to the palace.

What did the Babylonians do to Jerusalem?

King Nebuchadnezzar and the Babylonians surrounded Jerusalem for four months. The Israelites were starving by the time the soldiers burst through the city walls. The soldiers destroyed Jerusalem and its great temple. They stole all the gold and silver, took the people away as slaves and captured their king. All this happened because the Israelites had disobeyed God.

Where did Daniel live when he was a young man?

Daniel and his friends were from Jerusalem, but they had been captured by King Nebuchadnezzar of Babylonia. They were forced to live at his court and change their names. But God made them wise and they became valued advisors at court.

Who was thrown into a fiery furnace?

King Nebuchadnezzar threw Daniel's friends into a fiery furnace because they refused to worship a gold statue. Daniel was busy at the palace when this happened. God sent an angel to protect the friends from the flames and they were unharmed. The king was so amazed that he ordered everyone to respect God.

Why was Daniel thrown into the lions' den?

Some of the leaders in Babylonia were jealous of Daniel. They tricked Darius, the new king, into passing a law that said everyone should pray only to him. The leaders caught Daniel praying to God and made Darius punish him by throwing him into a lions' den. But God stopped the lions from harming Daniel. Darius was overjoyed, and he threw Daniel's enemies into the lions' den instead.

What happened when Jonah tried to run away from God?

God told Jonah to go to Nineveh to tell the people to obey God. But Jonah got on a boat going in the opposite direction. Then God raised a great storm. Jonah told the sailors it was his fault for running away, so they threw him overboard and he was swallowed alive by a great fish.

How long was Jonah in the belly of the fish?

God sent the great fish to swallow Jonah so that he did not drown. Jonah survived in its belly for three days and three nights. He prayed to God all the time, until at last God spoke to the fish and ordered it to spit out Jonah on to dry land.

Where did Jonah go when the big fish spat him out?

After Jonah was washed up on the beach, God told him again to go to Nineveh. This time Jonah obeyed, and he told the people of Nineveh that their city would be destroyed in forty days. The people believed that God would destroy their city, and they were very worried.

What happened to the people of Nineveh?

After Jonah had passed on God's message, the king of Nineveh told his people to stop eating to show that they were sorry for disobeying God. God saw that the people were truly sorry and forgave them. Their great city was not destroyed.

The Birth of Jesus

Who told Mary that she was going to have a baby?

The angel Gabriel came to Mary and told her that she was blessed by God, and that she was going to have a baby boy, whose name would be Jesus. Mary said that she would do whatever God expected of her.

Where was Jesus, the Son of God, born?

At the time her baby was due to be born, Mary and Joseph had to travel to Bethlehem. No rooms were left for them to stay in, but an innkeeper offered them his stable. Jesus was born there that night.

Who were the first visitors to see the baby Jesus?

After Jesus was born, an angel appeared to some shepherds who were guarding sheep on the hills. The angel said that a special baby had been born, and that they would find him in a manger in Bethlehem. The shepherds were scared at first, but they soon set off to visit Jesus.

Who else travelled a long way to see Jesus?

Wise men from the east saw a bright star in the sky. They knew this was a sign that a special child had been born, so they followed it. They found Jesus in Bethlehem, and gave him gifts of gold, frankincense and myrrh. King Herod asked them where the baby was, but the wise men knew he wished to harm Jesus, so they did not tell him.

What happened to Jesus at eight days old?

When Jesus was eight days old, he was circumcised in the Temple according to Jewish Law. Simeon and Anna were there. They had been faithfully waiting to see the holy child for many years. Simeon held Jesus, and blessed Mary and Joseph.

Who did Jesus amaze when he was twelve?

Mary and Joseph were travelling home from celebrating Passover in Jerusalem, when they realized Jesus was missing. They went back, and found him talking to teachers in the Temple. Everyone there was amazed by how much he understood. When Mary told Jesus that she had been worried, he said, "Did you not know I would be in my Father's house?"

Who did Jesus ask to baptize him?

John the Baptist was sent by God to warn people to change their ways and be baptized so God would forgive them. Jesus did not need God's forgiveness, but he asked John to baptize him in the River Jordan. God was pleased, and sent the Holy Spirit in the form of a dove.

How did Satan test Jesus in the desert?

When Jesus was hungry, Satan tested his obedience to God by asking him to turn stones into bread. Satan also asked Jesus to throw himself off the roof of the Temple to prove his power. Finally, Satan told Jesus he could have all the kingdoms in the world if he would worship only him. But Jesus loved God and refused to be tempted, and Satan eventually left him alone.

FRIENDS AND DISCIPLES

Who killed John the Baptist?

King Herod sent John to prison because John disapproved of his marriage to Herodias, his brother Philip's wife. When Herodias's daughter Salome danced for him, the king was so pleased that he promised her anything she wanted. Herodias told Salome to ask for John's head on a platter, so Herod had to have John killed.

How did Jesus meet his first disciples?

Jesus was preaching by Lake Galilee when he met Simon. Simon had been fishing all night without success, but Jesus got into his boat and told him to sail into deep water and start fishing again. Simon did as he was asked and soon his nets were bursting with fish. Simon, his brother Andrew, and James and John were astonished at what they saw. Jesus asked them to be his disciples and they all agreed.

How many disciples did Jesus have altogether?

Jesus had twelve disciples, who travelled with him. He taught them and gave them powers to heal people. They were Simon, who Jesus renamed Peter, his brother Andrew, James and John the sons of Zebedee, Philip, Bartholomew, Matthew, Thomas, James the son of Alphaeus, Thaddaeus, Simon the Zealot and Judas Iscariot.

What miracle did Jesus perform at a wedding in Cana?

Jesus and his disciples went to a wedding in Cana, to which Jesus' mother Mary had also been invited. When Mary told her son that the wine had run out, Jesus asked the servants to fill six large stone jars to the brim with water. Then he told them to take some of the water to the organizer of the feast. When this man tasted the water, it had turned into delicious wine. Jesus' disciples were amazed at this miracle, and their faith in him grew even stronger.

How was a woman of great faith healed by Jesus?

A woman in Capernaum had been ill for twelve years. When she saw Jesus, she reached through the crowd, touched his cloak, and was instantly healed. Jesus felt her touch, and when he turned to her she said, "I knew that if I touched your cloak I would be healed." Jesus told the woman that it was her faith that had cured her.

What miracle did Jesus perform on Lazarus?

Martha and Mary asked Jesus to visit their brother Lazarus, who was ill. By the time Jesus got there, Lazarus had already died and been buried. Jesus went to Lazarus' tomb and told him to come out and, to everyone's amazement, he did. Jesus had brought him back to life.

What lesson did Jesus teach about helping other people?

Jesus said that, in everything we do, we should show that we love one another. This means that we should treat other people in exactly the same way that we would like them to treat us. Jesus said that this important rule sums up the teaching of the prophets and of the Jewish Law.

How did Jesus say people should treat their enemies?

Jesus taught that we should love our neighbours. This means we should love and pray for our enemies as well as our friends. He said that it was easy to love our friends and family, but not so easy to love our enemies.

What did Jesus say could be learned from the flowers of the field?

Jesus said that the flowers of the field could teach us not to worry about things like clothes and money. Flowers do not worry about how they will live because God looks after all their needs. Because God loves us so much, everything we need will also be provided for us.

What special prayer did Jesus teach to his followers?

The prayer, known as the Lord's Prayer, praises God as Father on earth and in Heaven, and asks us to live in ways that please God. The prayer asks for God's blessing and forgiveness, reminds us to forgive others for their sins against us and asks that we be kept safe from temptation.

How did Jesus teach the people?

Jesus told stories about things that ordinary people were familiar with, such as families, farming and money. These stories, or parables, helped people to understand Jesus' special teaching about God.

Why did the lost son decide to go back home?

Jesus told a story in which he said that God was like a father welcoming back a lost son. The son asked his father for some money, then left home and spent it all. When the money was gone, he became lonely, hungry and unhappy. He knew he would rather be his father's servant than starving among strangers, so he went home. His father forgave him and welcomed him with open arms.

What kind thing did the Good Samaritan do?

Jesus told the story of a man from Samaria who stopped to help a traveller who had been robbed and beaten. While other people just walked past because they did not want to get involved, the Samaritan tended to the man's wounds. Jesus said that, unlike the other passers-by, the Samaritan was a good neighbour to the injured man.

AN INCREDIBLE PICNIC

How did Jesus feed more than five thousand people?

Thousands of people gathered together and stood for a whole day listening to Jesus preaching. By the end of the day the people were hungry, so Jesus told his disciples to feed them. The disciples said that they would need six months' wages to buy enough food for everyone, and that the only food available was one boy's picnic lunch of five small bread rolls and two dried fishes. Jesus told the crowd to sit down on the grass, then he blessed the bread and fishes, gave thanks to God and asked his disciples to give the food to the crowd. Amazingly, there was plenty for everyone.

What did the disciples do after everyone had eaten?

When the crowd had eaten their fill, Jesus told his disciples to collect everything that was left over from the incredible picnic of bread and fishes. There was enough left to fill twelve baskets. The crowd was amazed by this miracle and the people began to say that Jesus was a great prophet.

What happened on Lake Galilee?

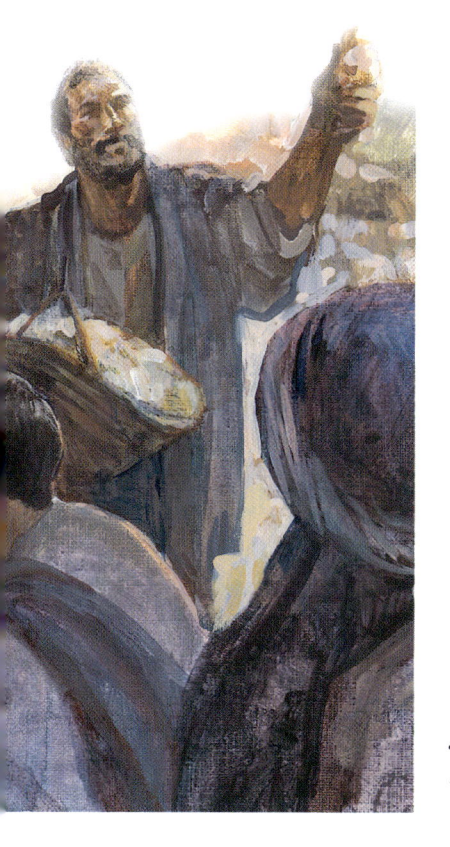

The disciples were in a boat on Lake Galilee when they saw Jesus walking towards them on the water. They thought he was a ghost at first, but Jesus told them not to be afraid. Peter got out of the boat and walked across the water towards Jesus, but then he panicked and began to sink. Jesus said, "Why did you doubt me?" Then he reached out his hand and saved him.

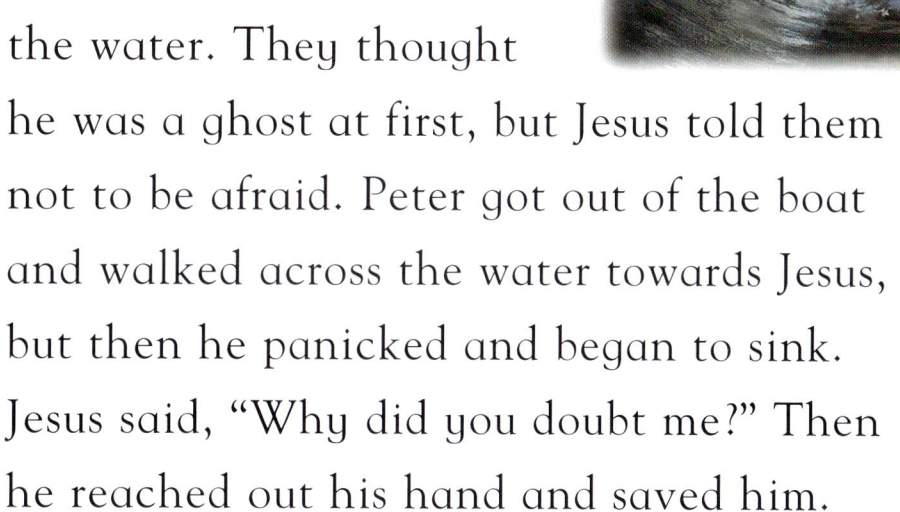

How did Jesus travel into Jerusalem before the Passover?

Prophets said that God would send someone to help the people, and that he would ride a donkey. Jesus wanted everyone to know he was that special person, so he rode a donkey into Jerusalem.

How was Jesus welcomed into Jerusalem?

The people were very excited because they thought that Jesus would be a mighty king. They cheered, and some of them put their coats on the ground in front of him and waved palm branches.

What did Jesus do in the Temple in Jerusalem?

Jesus overturned tables and stalls that were being used by money-lenders and people selling animals for sacrifice. He then healed sick people, who had heard what was going on and had come to see him. The people loved Jesus, and this made the priests jealous.

Why was Jesus so angry when he visited the Temple?

Jesus was angry with the priests for allowing people to use the Temple for making money, instead of for worshipping God and praying. He drove the market-traders away and shouted at the priests, saying that the Temple should be called a house of prayer, and that they had instead turned it into a den of thieves.

What was the Last Supper?

All Jews ate a Passover meal each year to remember the time when God freed them from Egypt and saved their children from death. Jesus and his disciples met to eat that meal together. It was the last meal that they all shared before Jesus died.

What did Jesus do for his followers before they ate?

Jesus washed his disciples' feet to set an example for them to follow. Even though he was their leader, he was prepared to serve them. He told them that they should be ready to do the same for others.

The Last Supper

What was special about the food and drink at the Last Supper?

Jesus broke some bread and poured some wine. He blessed the food and drink, and gave it to his disciples. He said that when they shared bread and wine in the future, it would remind them of his coming death. His body would be broken like the bread, and his blood would be spilt like the wine.

What new commandment did Jesus ask his disciples to obey?

Jesus said that, when he was gone, he wanted people to live as he did, helping others and showing love for everyone. But the disciples then began to argue with each other about which one of them was the most important. Jesus told them that the only important thing was that they should love one another just as he had loved them. He said that, if they did as he said, everyone would know that they were disciples of Jesus.

TRIAL AND CRUCIFIXION

Who betrayed Jesus to his enemies?

Judas Iscariot was one of the disciples, but he betrayed Jesus for thirty pieces of silver. Judas led soldiers to the Garden of Gethsemane and showed them who Jesus was by greeting him with a kiss. The soldiers arrested Jesus and took him away for questioning.

Which disciple said three times that he was not Jesus' friend?

Peter was a loyal friend to Jesus most of the time, but he became very afraid when Jesus was arrested. When people in Jerusalem said that he was a friend of Jesus, he denied it three times so that he would not be arrested. After Peter denied Jesus for the third time, a cock crowed. This was exactly what Jesus had said would happen.

How did Jesus die?

The Roman governor Pontius Pilate sentenced Jesus to death by crucifixion. Soldiers took him away and whipped him. They dressed him in a cloak and put a crown of thorns upon his head. They mocked him by calling him the King of the Jews. Then they made Jesus carry his heavy wooden cross to a place called Golgotha, outside the city walls. He was so weak that he could not carry it all the way, and a man called Simon of Cyrene carried it for him. When they arrived, soldiers nailed Jesus on to the wooden cross. He was in great pain for hours before he died.

THE RESURRECTION

Where was Jesus buried?

Joseph of Arimathea asked Pontius Pilate for Jesus' body so that he could bury him. He wrapped the body in linen burial clothes and put it in his own rock tomb in a garden. Then he rolled a heavy stone in front of the entrance. The authorities sent soldiers to guard the tomb because they thought that someone might try to steal the body.

What did Mary Magdalene and her friend Mary find in Jesus' tomb?

The day after Jesus was buried, the two Marys went to his tomb. They found that the heavy stone had been rolled aside. The tomb was empty except for two bits of cloth. The cloth that had been wrapped around Jesus' body was in one place, and the cloth that had covered his head was in another. Jesus' body was not there.

How did Jesus show that he had risen from the dead?

After Jesus rose from the dead, he met and talked to his disciples several times. He ate with them, and once he even cooked a meal of fish for them. He showed them the holes that the nails had made in his hands and feet, and a hole that a Roman soldier's spear had made in his side. In all, Jesus showed himself to more than five hundred people so that they knew he had risen from the dead.

What did Jesus tell his friends before he returned to Heaven?

Jesus taught his disciples many more things about God before he left them. He said he would send the Holy Spirit to help them live in ways that pleased God, and told them to spread all over the world the good news that he had risen from death. Jesus promised his disciples that, although he was going to Heaven, he would always be with them.

What happened to Jesus' followers?

One day after Jesus had returned to Heaven, the disciples met together, and Jesus sent the Holy Spirit to help them to do God's work. They heard a sound like rushing wind, and it seemed as if tongues of fire touched them. This was when they received the power of the Holy Spirit of God. Then they were able to preach in many languages so that everyone understood them.

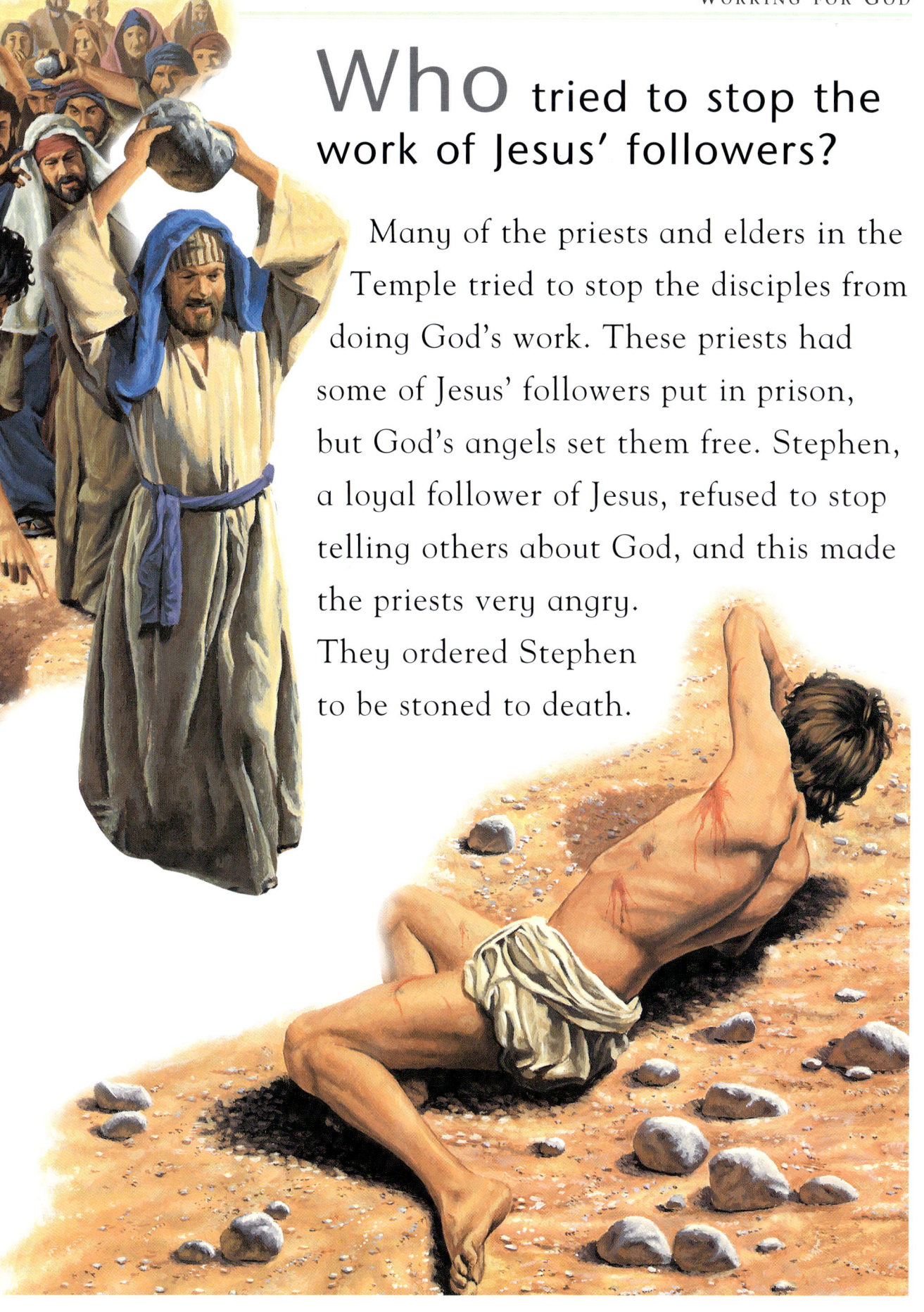

Who tried to stop the work of Jesus' followers?

Many of the priests and elders in the Temple tried to stop the disciples from doing God's work. These priests had some of Jesus' followers put in prison, but God's angels set them free. Stephen, a loyal follower of Jesus, refused to stop telling others about God, and this made the priests very angry. They ordered Stephen to be stoned to death.

PAUL THE APOSTLE

What made Saul change his ways and become a servant of God?

Saul was one of those who tried to stop the work of Jesus' followers, but God wanted to use him to teach people about Jesus. On the road to Damascus, Saul was blinded by a bright light from Heaven. Then he heard Jesus telling him to go to Damascus and wait. In the city, a man called Ananias healed Saul's blindness. After that, Saul believed that Jesus had risen from death, and decided to follow him.

Why did Paul travel to many different countries?

Some years after Saul's conversion, he became known as Paul. God asked him to tell as many people as possible about Jesus. So Paul travelled to many countries teaching people about Jesus and explaining God's message. He showed them how to worship together and praise God.

What happened to Paul on his way to Rome?

Paul was put in prison many times. Once, he was imprisoned in a ship going to Rome, but on the way it was wrecked in a storm. Everyone survived, and Paul continued teaching about God. He wrote to the new churches, encouraging them to follow what he had taught them.

Index

A
Abel 9
Abraham 12–13
Absalom 31
Adam 6–9
Alphaeus 43
Andrew 42–43
angels 15, 23, 34, 38, 39, 61
ark, Noah's 10
Ark of the Covenant 24, 27, 31, 32

B
Baal 33
Babylonia 34, 35
Babylonians 33
baptism 41
Bethel 15
Bethlehem 38, 39
Bible 31
big fish 36–37
bread 55
burning bush 19

C
Cain 9
Cana 44
Canaan 15, 26
Canaanites 28
Capernaum 45
circumcision 40
Creation 6–7
cross 57
crown of thorns 57
crucifixion 57

D
Damascus 62
Daniel 34–35
Darius, King 35
David 30–32
Deborah 28
disciples 42, 43, 44, 50, 51, 54–55, 56, 59, 60–61
donkey 52
dove 10, 41
dreams 17

E, F
Eden 7–8
Egypt 17, 18, 20–22, 54
Egyptians 18–19, 20, 21, 22, 23
Eli 29
Elijah 33
Esau 14
Eve 6–9
fish 36–37, 42, 50, 59
flood 10–11

G, H
Gabriel, angel 38
Galilee, Lake 42, 51
Garden of Gethsemane 56
Golgotha 57
Goliath 30
Good Samaritan 49
Heaven 15, 60, 62
Herod 39, 42
Holy Spirit 41, 60

I, J
Isaac 12, 13, 14
Israel 15, 28, 29, 31
Israelites 18–19, 20–27, 28–30, 33
Jacob 14, 15, 16
James 42, 43
Jericho 26–27
Jerusalem 31, 32, 33, 34, 40, 52, 53, 56
Jesus 38–63
John 42, 43
John the Baptist 41, 42
Jonah 36–37
Joseph 16, 17, 18, 38, 40
Joshua 26, 27
Judas Iscariot 43, 56

K, L
kiss, Judas 56
Last Supper 54–55
Lazarus 45
lions' den 35
Lord's Prayer 47

M, N
manger 39
Mary 38, 40, 44, 45
Mary Magdalene 58
Matthew 43
miracles 27, 44–45, 51
Miriam 18
Moses 18–20, 22, 24–26
Mother of Israel 28
Nebuchadnezzar, King 33–34
Nineveh 36–37
Noah 10–11

P
parables 48
Passover 21–22, 40, 52, 54
Paul 63
Peter 43, 51, 56
pharaohs 17, 19–23
Philip 43
Philistines 29, 30
plagues 20–21, 22, 25
Pontius Pilate 57, 58
Potiphar 17
Promised Land 26

R
rainbow 11
Rebecca 13, 14
Red Sea 22, 23
Resurrection 58–59
River Jordan 41
River Nile 18
Romans 57, 59

S
Sabbath 7, 24
sacrifice 12–13, 53
Salome 42
Samson 29
Samuel 29
Sarah 12
Satan 41
Saul 62–63
Saul, King 30
shepherds 39
Simeon 40
Simon 42, 43
Simon of Cyrene 57
Simon the Zealot 43
slavery 16, 17, 18, 19
Solomon 32
Stephen 61

T
Tabernacle 24
Temple 32, 33, 40, 41, 53, 61
Ten Commandments 24–25
Thaddaeus 43
Thomas 43
tomb 58
tongues of fire 60

U, W, Z
unrisen bread 22
walking on water 51
wine 44, 55
wise men 39
Zebedee 43

FURTHER READING
GENESIS: The Creation; Noah and the flood; Abraham and Isaac; Jacob; Joseph
EXODUS: Moses; plagues in Egypt; the Israelites; The Ten Commandments
JOSHUA: The Promised Land
JUDGES: Deborah; Gideon; Samson; Samuel
SAMUEL I AND II: David
KINGS I AND II: King Solomon; Elijah; King Nebuchadnezzar
DANIEL: Daniel
JONAH: Jonah and the big fish
MATTHEW, MARK, LUKE AND JOHN: The life of Jesus
ACTS: The Holy Spirit comes; Paul the apostle